inside
GADGETS

By Steve Parker
Illustrated by Alex Pang

Miles Kelly

First published in 2009 by Miles Kelly Publishing Ltd
Harding's Barn, Bardfield End Green, Thaxted, Essex, CM6 3PX, UK

This edition printed in 2012

10 9 8 7 6 5 4 3 2 1

Publishing Director: *Belinda Gallagher*
Creative Director: *Jo Cowan*
Design Concept: *Simon Lee*
Volume Design: *Rocket Design*
Cover Designer: *Simon Lee*
Indexer: *Gill Lee*
Production Manager: *Elizabeth Collins*
Reprographics: *Stephan Davis, Thom Allaway*
Consultants: *John and Sue Becklake*
Edition Editor: *Amanda Askew*

ISBN 978-1-84810-835-6

Printed in China

British Library Cataloguing-in-Publication Data
A catalogue record for this book is available from the British Library

Every effort has been made to acknowledge the source and copyright
holder of each picture. Miles Kelly Publishing apologises for any
unintentional errors or omissions.

MADE WITH PAPER FROM
A SUSTAINABLE FOREST

ACKNOWLEDGEMENTS

All panel artworks by Rocket Design
The publishers would like to thank the following sources
for the use of their photographs:
Corbis: 6(t/r) Carl & Ann Purcell; 14 TScI/NASA/Roger
Ressmeyer; 16 Reuters; 22 Ed Kashi
Fotolia: 6(c) Avava; 7(t) Henrik Andersen;
25 Monkey Business; 27 Peter Baxter; 35 Andy Dean
Rex Features: 28 Action Press; 30 c.W.Disney/Everett
Science Photo Library: 20 James King-Holmes;
37 David Hay Jones
Shutterstock: COVER Andresr, Brett Mulcahy; 7(r)
Barone Firenze; 8 Torsten Lorenz; 11 Fedorov Oleksiy;
32 Jordan Tam
All other photographs are from Miles Kelly Archives

WWW.FACTSFORPROJECTS.COM

Each top right-hand page directs
you to the Internet to help you
find out more. You can log on
to **www.factsforprojects.com**
to find free pictures, additional
information, videos, fun activities
and further web links. These
are for your own personal use
and should not be copied or
distributed for any commercial
or profit-related purpose.

If you do decide to use the
Internet with your book, here's a
list of what you'll need:
• A PC with Microsoft® Windows®
XP or later versions, or a
Macintosh with OS X or later,
and 512Mb RAM

• A browser such as Microsoft®
Internet Explorer 9, Firefox 4.X
or Safari 5.X
• Connection to the Internet.
Broadband connection
recommended.
• An account with an Internet
Service Provider (ISP)
• A sound card for listening to
sound files

Links won't work?
www.factsforprojects.com is
regularly checked to make sure
the links provide you with lots
of information. Sometimes you
may receive a message saying
that a site is unavailable. If this
happens, just try again later.

Stay safe!
When using the Internet, make
sure you follow these guidelines:
• Ask a parent's or a guardian's
permission before you log on.
• Never give out your personal
details, such as your name,
address or email.
• If a site asks you to log in or
register by typing your name
or email address, speak to your
parent or guardian first.
• If you do receive an email from
someone you don't know, tell
an adult and do not reply to the
message.
• Never arrange to meet anyone
you have talked to on the
Internet.

www.mileskelly.net
info@mileskelly.net

CONTENTS

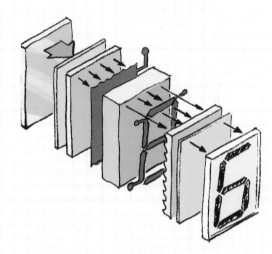

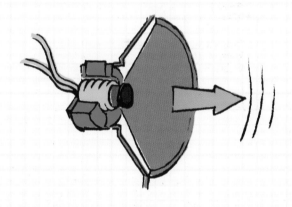

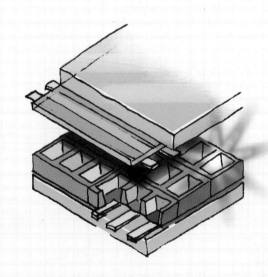

INTRODUCTION

People have always loved gadgets. In ancient times, alongside important tools and machines such as levers and wheels, people also invented gadgets, gizmos, widgets and devices to make life easier and more fun. Many gadgets were novelties that came and went, used just for entertainment. But others took on more serious uses and became part of everyday life, such as the abacus, alarm clock and microwave oven.

A skilled abacus user can work out sums almost as fast as a skilled electronic calculator user.

HIGHER TECH

The story of gadgets follows the march of technology. The calculator began thousands of years ago as rows of pebbles, then wooden beads on wires, followed by hand-cranked mechanical versions, and then an electric motor design. From the 1940s, electronics and microchips not only shrank the calculator to pocket size but also started a whole new area for gizmology. It has led to the ultimate gadget of our times – the computer.

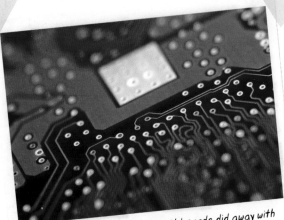

Mass-produced printed circuit boards did away with the labour-intensive task of installing wires by hand.

Personal music players are small enough to be carried wherever we go.

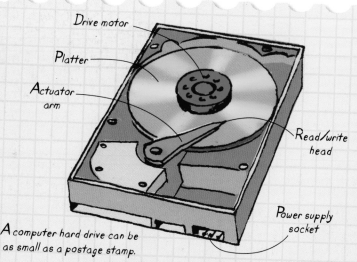

Drive motor

Platter

Actuator arm

Read/write head

Power supply socket

A computer hard drive can be as small as a postage stamp.

SMALL IS BIG

The market for new gadgets seems endless. Adverts continually announce smaller size, less weight, better batteries, easier controls and more add-ons and features. Sometimes existing parts are miniaturized for a new use, like the micro versions of computer hard drives developed for personal music players. In other cases a different area of technology is devised, such as 'flash' digital memory sticks or pens for music players.

The gadgets featured in this book are Internet linked.
Visit www.factsforprojects.com to find out more.

Wide open spaces are recorded by a camcorder microchip smaller than your fingernail.

SIZE MATTERS

Some technologies resist the shrinking trend. Optical or light-based gadgets such as cameras and camcorders have to be a certain size, otherwise they could not handle enough light rays from the real world to record and show us the scene.

Manipulating light rays makes things look nearer or farther.

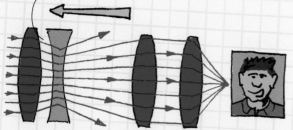

Concave lens to front

Camera zoom lens at telephoto setting

Concave lens to rear

Camera zoom lens at wide-angle setting

NO LIMITS?

Will there come a time when all possible gadgets have been invented? That's very doubtful. Few people 25 years ago predicted the success of sports-playing computers that keep you active, brain-training video consoles, car satnavs and internet-enabled, do-everything mobile phones. What will the next 25 years bring? Perhaps a new generation of plug-in brain chips, a TV screen fitted inside the eyeball and thought-wave communicators.

We can be sure of one thing – people will always want the most cutting-edge gadgets, so the well-worn phrase "I want one of those" will always survive!

There are even gadgets to cause you brain strain, such as this Nintendo DS gaming device.

CALCULATOR

Long ago, people did sums and calculations with pencil and paper, or used a machine as big as a table with lots of gears – or in their heads. In the 1960s came hand-held calculators, which were among the first small electronic gadgets. Today they are found in almost every room in offices, schools, factories and homes.

Eureka!

A calculating machine called the abacus was used in ancient Greece and Rome over 2000 years ago. It had rows of pebbles or beads in grooves on a table or in sand.

Whatever next?

Scientists are testing foldable calculators, with the keys and display built into thin, flexible cloth like a small handkerchief.

Microchips are also called ICs, integrated circuits, because they contain microscopic components, such as transistors and resistors, already 'integrated' on one wafer-like chip of silicon.

Cover The outer cover is usually made of hard plastic, able to resist scratches and knocks.

✳ PORTABLE POWER

Early calculators had LED (light-emitting diode) displays that needed plenty of battery power. With the introduction of LCD screens, which use much less electricity, enough power for a small calculator could be provided by a photovoltaic cell, or solar cell, which turns light energy into electricity. Most modern gadgets have built-in secondary electrical cells – rechargeable batteries that can be plugged into the mains.

PCB (Printed Circuit Board) Electronic components are linked by metal strips 'printed' onto a board made of a green plastic-like substance that is an electrical insulator (does not carry electricity).

Microprocessor The 'brain' of any electronic device is a chip called the microprocessor, or CPU, central processing unit. It carries out calculations from instructions fed into it via the keys.

Batteries range in size from smaller than a button to bigger than a suitcase

The most complex microprocessors or CPUs have more than ten million components on a chip as small as this 'o'.

To find out more about LCD and how it works visit www.factsforprojects.com and click on the web link.

Display window

CASIO SCIENTIFIC CALCULATOR fx-250c

Specialist calculators are used in many areas of science, engineering and even sport. They can work out the amounts of materials needed to build a skyscraper, predict the weather or tell you how much air you have left when scuba-diving.

LCD The liquid crystal display can be backlit for dim conditions, rather than using reflected daylight. However the backlight uses more electricity than the display itself.

Rubber pads

Keys The usual numerical keys have standard positions. There is also a row of arithmetical function keys, usually on the right, to add, subtract, divide and multiply.

Ribbon connector

DURACELL POWERCHECK

How do LCDs work?

A liquid crystal can polarize light rays, 'twisting' them so they undulate (go up and down) at the same angle, depending on whether electricity flows through them. Switched off, daylight enters the LCD at the front, goes through all the layers, bounces off the rear mirror and comes back out. Switched on, the liquid crystal polarizes all the light rays into one certain angle. Two other polarizing layers at the opposite angle then block these rays completely. No light can come back out, and the display then looks dark.

Rear mirror

Polarizing film

Negative electrode (electrical contact)

Positive electrode (electrical contact)

Polarizing film

Glass

Liquid crystal layer

Glass

Glass cover with displayed image

Battery compartment Longlife or rechargeable batteries are needed for bigger calculators used for long periods, especially in dim conditions where a solar cell could not supply enough electricity.

Back panel

FLAT SCREEN

Flat screens are in computer monitors, TVs and closed-circuit TV, displays on digital cameras, camcorders, satnav units and phones, and many other devices. There are two main kinds of flat screen technology – LCD (see page 9) and plasma (see below). Flat screens took over in the 1990s from older, heavier, box-like, glass-screen displays known as CRTs, cathode ray tubes. A CRT uses far more electricity than a flat screen.

Eureka!

The first purely electronic television systems, with no moving parts, were developed in the 1920s–30s by Hungarian engineer Kalman Tihanyi and Russian-American inventor Vladimir Zworykin.

Clear cover

✳ How do PLASMA SCREENS work?

A plasma screen has millions of tiny compartments or cells, and two sets or grids of wire-like electrodes at right angles to each other. Each cell can be 'addressed' by sending electric pulses along two particular electrodes that cross at the cell. The electric pulse heats the cell's gas into a form called plasma, and this makes an area of coloured substance, the phosphor, glow for a split second. Millions of pulses every second at different 'addresses' all over the screen build up the overall picture.

Screen format Most flat screens have a 16:9 aspect ratio for widescreen viewing, where the screen height is 9/16ths of its width.

Remote sensor A small infrared sensor detects the invisible IR (heat) beam from the remote-control handset.

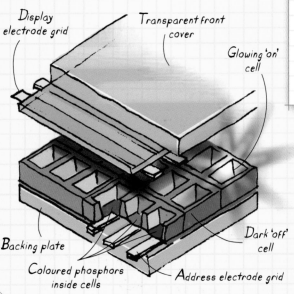

Display electrode grid

Transparent front cover

Glowing 'on' cell

Backing plate

Coloured phosphors inside cells

Dark 'off' cell

Address electrode grid

Stand

The biggest LCD flat screens measure 108 in or 274 cms. That's the distance from corner to corner diagonally across the screen, which is the traditional way of sizing screens.

In 1925, Scottish inventor John Logie Baird built a part-mechanical TV system, used by the BBC from 1929–1937.

Whatever next?

HD or High Definition screens have five to six times more tiny coloured dots (pixels) than a standard flat screen. This gives a sharper, clearer, more colourful image and smoother, less jerky movements.

Read all about High Definition TV by visiting www.factsforprojects.com and clicking on the web link.

The QuadHD flat screen has four to five times as many tiny coloured dots (pixels) than an HD flat screen – but whether most people have good enough eyesight to tell the difference is unlikely.

Receiver A TV's receiver unit is part of the electronic circuit board. It tunes into different channels and filters and strengthens the signals received by the aerial, ready for electronic processing. Computer monitors receive their signals already processed and so lack a receiver.

Ventilation slots The outer casing needs slots at the rear to allow heat to escape, otherwise the thermal cutout makes the screen go blank to prevent components overheating.

Electronics A typical HD flat screen TV has more than 1000 microchips and other components.

Most LCD flat screens use TFTs, thin-film transistors. The transistor components for producing coloured dots in the pixels are made within the thickness of the transparent screen.

✳ DIGITAL BROADCASTING

Older television broadcasting was called analogue, where the information for the pictures and sounds was carried by the varying strength of the radio wave signals. In digital broadcasting the information is coded in the form of on-off signals, millions every second. Radio waves used for one analogue channel can carry up to ten digital channels.

Frame and backing The outer frame keeps the screen rigid and secure and wraps around the electronics at the rear. Some flat screens are less than 2.5 cm deep.

Dishes receive digital signals direct from satellites in space

PERSONAL COMPUTER

Since the 1970s, personal computers have progressed from machines as big as a fridge that only the wealthy could afford, to small, neat packages found on and under desks in almost every home. A 'personal' computer, or PC, is usually stand-alone, which means it works by itself without being connected into a network with shared devices such as servers and other computers.

Eureka!

The first successful personal computer was the Commodore PET (Personal Electronic Transactor) in 1972. IBM's home computer, the IBM PC, was introduced in 1981 and set the standard for the computing industry.

Whatever next?

Moore's Law says that computer power – the number of components on a microchip and how fast they work – doubles about every two years. Devised by Gordon Moore in 1965, it is still holding true today.

Many modern computers have wireless peripherals (connected devices) that use short-range radio waves, such as the Bluetooth system, to carry information. This gets rid of trailing wires and allows them to be moved easily.

CPU The Central Processing Unit, or computer's 'brain', is connected to several other microchips. It carries out the main processing – altering data (information) according to the instructions from the application (program).

Cooling fan

RAM (Random Access Memory) chips

Card Smaller PCBs known as 'cards' deal with signals going in and out, for example, to the display screen from the graphics card, and to the loudspeakers from the sound card.

Hard drive The main memory disc that stores information permanently as micro-spots of magnetism is known as the hard disc or hard drive (see page 26).

✳ How do KEYBOARDS work?

All kinds of press-button or key-activated gadgets, from mobile phones to super computers, rely on a simple piece of technology similar to a light switch. Under each key are two pieces of metal conductor separated by a small gap. Pressing the key pushes them together so electricity flows. Each key has its own code of electrical pulses. A flexible membrane cover keeps out dust and sometimes even spilt drinks.

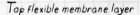

Top flexible membrane layer

Conductive strips not touching, 'open' circuit

Finger presses down on keypad

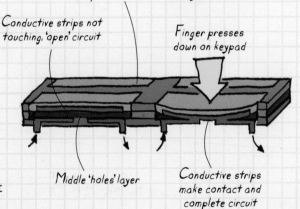

Middle 'holes' layer

Conductive strips make contact and complete circuit

Motherboard The main PCB (printed circuit board), which carries most of the major microchips, and the connectors for other, smaller PCBs, is often called the motherboard.

For information on computing history plus a game to play visit www.factsforprojects.com and click on the web link.

Optical drive trays CDs (compact discs) and DVDs (digital versatile discs) are inserted here where they work using light. A laser beam 'reads' tiny pits in their shiny surfaces (see page 31).

A typical home computer costs one-quarter of its price 20 years ago – and it is ten times more powerful.

Flat screen monitor

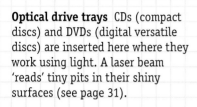

✳ The INTERNET

The global system of computers linked into an international network is known as the Internet. It began as a limited network for the US military in 1969, was widened to research centres and universities in the 1970s, taken up by businesses in the 1980s, and opened for public access in the 1990s.

Pages and documents viewed on the Internet form the World Wide Web.

IBM's 'Roadrunner', located at Los Alamos National Laboratory in New Mexico, USA, is currently the world's fastest super computer.

Mouse A laser beam or a rolling ball on the underside track the movements of the mouse. This makes the cursor or insertion point on the screen move in a similar way. The wireless mouse works by a Bluetooth short-wave radio link and so has no wire 'tail'.

Keyboard This is the main input device, allowing information to enter the computer as codes for alphanumerics – letters, numbers and symbols such as + and &.

Home computing did not really catch on until early games machines appeared such as the Atari 2600 (1977) and Sinclair ZX Spectrum (1982). They could play games in full colour and with sound – amazing for the time!

DIGITAL CAMERA

A camera makes a permanent visual record of a scene, person or object. Most cameras have a lens to focus the light rays for a clear image. A digital stills camera (recording a 'still' split-second moment in time) turns the pattern of light rays into on-off electronic signals stored in a microchip.

Eureka!

Early digital cameras included the Fuji DS-1P of 1988 and the Dycam M1 of 1990. Kodak introduced its first digi-cam in 1991 with the DCS-100.

Whatever next?

Early digital cameras recorded images of about one megapixel. For a typical camera in the 2000s this rose to six megapixels, then eight. It will continue to rise as CCD chips improve.

Digital cameras may not capture such detail or colour variation as photographic film cameras. However they can show you the image being stored, delete it if need be and hold many more images than a roll of film.

Autofocus An invisible infrared beam bounces off the object in front of the camera, which detects the time taken for it to return. This shows the object's distance for lens focusing.

Aperture This hole is made larger or smaller to let in more or less light, depending on brightness conditions.

'Take' button

✳ MEGAPIXELS and RESOLUTION

A megapixel is one million pixels, and pixels, or 'picture elements', are tiny areas or spots in the whole picture. Each pixel is made up of red, green and blue light. In various combinations these produce all other colours, and all together they make white. Packing more pixels into a given area makes the image clearer and more detailed, which is known as going from low resolution to high resolution.

Lens The lens system has several curved pieces of glass or plastic that move forwards or backwards to focus the image, depending on the object's distance.

A space galaxy at low resolution (left) and higher resolution (right)

Shutter Pressing the 'take' button opens a door-like flap for a split second to allow light through to the CCD (see page 18).

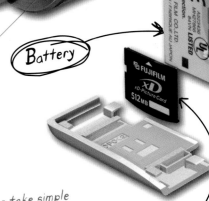

Battery

Memory card

Many digital cameras can take simple sequences of moving images or videos, and record sound too.

For lots of useful hints and tips on how to use your digital camera
go to www.factsforprojects.com and click on the web link.

A traditional camera stores images as patterns of silver-containing chemical changes on a flexible cellulose-based roll of photographic film.

Viewfinder A small LCD display shows the view that the lens sees, which is the image that will be stored.

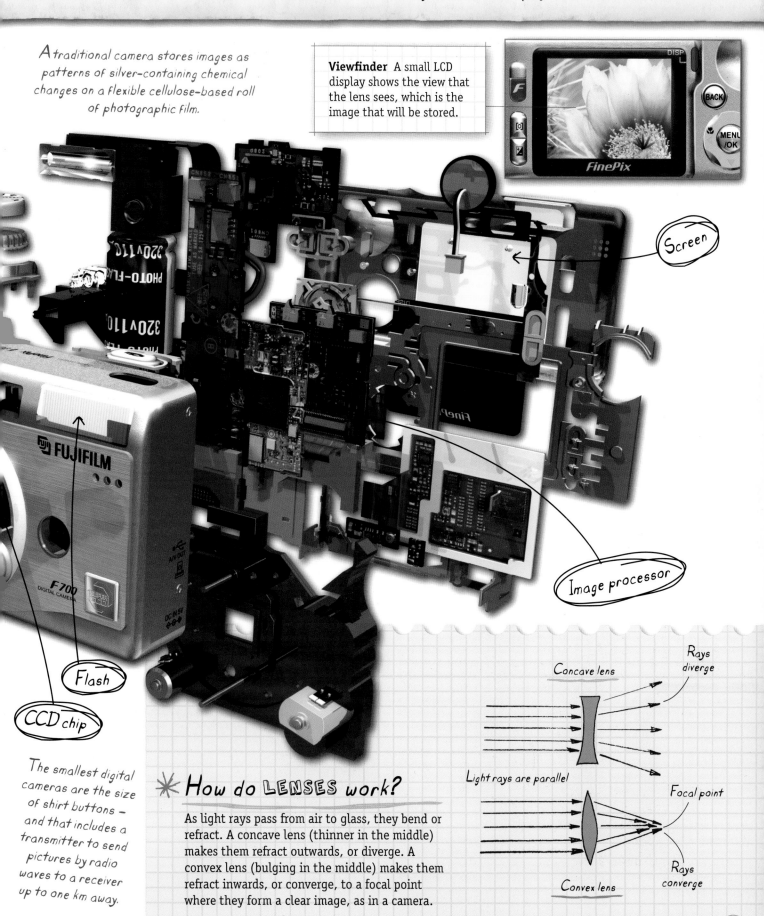

DISP

BACK

MENU /OK

FinePix

Screen

Image processor

Flash

CCD chip

FUJIFILM

F700
DIGITAL CAMERA

The smallest digital cameras are the size of shirt buttons – and that includes a transmitter to send pictures by radio waves to a receiver up to one km away.

✳ How do LENSES work?

As light rays pass from air to glass, they bend or refract. A concave lens (thinner in the middle) makes them refract outwards, or diverge. A convex lens (bulging in the middle) makes them refract inwards, or converge, to a focal point where they form a clear image, as in a camera.

Concave lens

Rays diverge

Light rays are parallel

Focal point

Convex lens

Rays converge

15

CAMCORDER

The camcorder is a camera-recorder specialized to take video – very fast split-second sequences of still images that look like moving pictures – and record them for later playback. It also records sounds at the time, which are linked in time, or synched (synchronized), to the images. Some camcorders record on magnetic tape, either analogue or digitally. Others are digital, using very small hard drives or electronic microchips in memory cards.

Eureka!

The first video cameras were cinema cameras using photographic film. Made in the 1880s, they recorded early movies or cinema 'motion pictures'. Small hand-held versions became popular from the 1950s.

Whatever next?

A light-detecting electronic chip that works as a simple video camera could one day be put into the eye, so you can make a permanent record of everything you see.

Zoom gears A small electric motor and gearing system move the lenses so that the camera can focus and zoom in to show a small area larger (see right).

Lens cover

Casing The scratchproof outer casing gives some protection against knocks.

Main processors The main microchips process the digital signals from the CCD into a form that is easily stored in the memory device.

✳ SATELLITE VIDEOPHONE

Satvidphones have a radio link, not into the local telecom or cellphone network as used by mobile phones, but direct to a satellite orbiting in space. The transmitter-receiver is housed in a laptop-sized case. A headset carries the camera to record the view, the microphone for sound and a display screen and headphones, either for what is being recorded, or to relay video and sound sent through the satellite link to the wearer.

The headset camera (left) records what is in front of the person's face

The highest-quality digital formats include MiniDV and Digital Betacam. They lose much less quality when the video recording is later copied and edited, compared to an analogue recording.

Create your own digital movie by visiting
www.factsforprojects.com and clicking on the web link.

Microphone A small microphone (see page 22) picks up sounds during image recording. On some cameras it can be detached for accurate aiming, linked to the camcorder by a wire or radio waves.

Early camcorders were developed for television, being small and lightweight for 'on-the-spot' reporting and recording.

Viewfinder The LCD screen allows you to see what has been recorded and delete it, or 'edit' it by picking out only the parts you want to save.

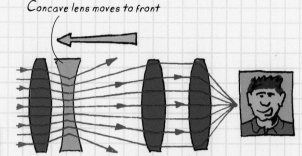
Concave lens moves to front
Zoom lens at telephoto setting

Concave lens moves to rear
Zoom lens at wide-angle setting

✳ How does ZOOM work?

Zooming in, or telephoto, enlarges a portion of the scene, at the same time showing a relatively smaller area of the whole scene. Zooming out to wide-angle takes in more of the scene but reduces its magnification so things look smaller. The zoom system uses a moveable concave lens (one that is thinner in the centre than around the edges) to spread out or diverge the light rays (see page 15). Some zooms are worked by an electric motor, others are twisted or pulled by hand.

Battery

USB memory stick

LCD display

Screen controls The screen has brightness, contrast, colour balance and other controls. You can adjust these to view it comfortably out in the glaring sunshine or indoors in a darkened room.

Most photographic film video cameras take 24 separate still pictures or frames every second. Camcorders usually take 30 frames per second. When the recording is played back, your eyes cannot see the individual frames separately. Your brain blurs them together to give the impression of smooth movement.

Webcams (World Wide Web cameras) are small, simple video cameras that do not record their images but feed them straight into a computer or digital network.

SCANNER

The key to digital technology is to turn anything – pictures, videos, sounds, speech, written words and numbers – into coded sequences of on-off electrical pulses. We write these as the digits (numbers) 1 and 0, and they are the 'language' of computers. An image scanner 'digitizes' a picture by detecting the colour and brightness of every tiny spot, one spot after another, and converting this information to digital code.

Eureka!

The first image scanners appeared in the 1960s, as part of the work to develop body scanners for medical use. They were taken up by businesses in the 1980s and became available for home use in the early 1990s.

Whatever next?

Three-dimensional (3D) scanners consist of two digital cameras mounted on a frame. They are moved over and around an object, to make a 3D view in the computer memory.

Drive motor housing

PCB

Drive gear

Scan technology involves looking at and detecting a row of tiny areas in a straight line, then moving along slightly and doing the same for the next line, and so on – usually thousands of times.

Light source A very bright light, as pure white as possible, shines onto the image. Its light rays reflect off the image with the colour and brightness of every part of that image.

Rail The scan head slides to and fro along a metal guide rail. It is driven by a toothed belt that meshes to a sprocket (gear wheel) for very accurate movement.

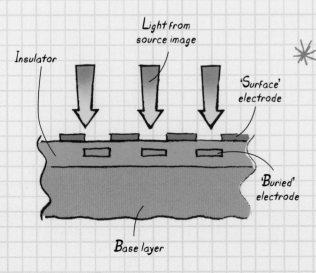

Light from source image

Insulator

'Surface' electrode

'Buried' electrode

Base layer

☀ How does a CCD CHIP work?

A CCD (charge-coupled device) is a microchip with millions of tiny wire-like electrodes forming a criss-cross grid. When a ray of light hits the area or boundary between two neighbouring electrodes, it causes a particle called an electron (an outer part of an atom) to jump between them. This causes a tiny pulse of electric current at that point on the chip – light has been converted into electricity.

Control buttons The scanner has some manual controls, such as to 'home' the scan head, to scan only a small area or to make a direct copy. Most of the controls are in the computer application to which it is linked.

For some great tips on scanning at home visit
www.factsforprojects.com and click on the web link.

The detail that a scanner picks up is measured as dpi, dots per inch. This shows how many dots of colour are detected in a line one inch (2.54 cm) long.

Tray

Direct output (copy)

If large areas of an image are the same colour, the computer can save memory by giving them all a shortened version of the code for that colour, rather than the full code for every tiny spot of the area. This is one way of compressing a computer file to make it smaller.

Sealed case The scanner's internal parts are sealed to keep them dust-proof, since build-up of dust on the mirrors, lenses and CCD would greatly affect the quality of the scan.

A red shirt is changed to blue – or the other way around?

Power button

Flatbed The image is laid flat on a glass sheet for flatbed scanning. Some scanners have a different design where the image is wrapped around a drum that revolves past the scan head. Drum scanners can produce a far more detailed scan.

Main housing Inside the scanner's main case is a mirror that reflects light that has already been reflected from the image. The mirror reflects the light towards the CCD, which turns the patterns of colour and brightness in the light rays into a corresponding pattern of electronic digital signals.

✳ VSFX

Using keyboard instructions, computers can change or process words. The same can be done with pictures, known as image processing or visual special effects (VSFX). For example, the computer can be instructed to change all areas of a certain shade of red in an image to a blue colour.

PRINTER

A typical home printer makes 'hard copy' – a version or copy of what is on the computer screen, on a sheet of paper or card where it is permanent or 'hard'. Printer technology is in some ways the opposite of the image scanner (see page 18). The printer builds up the image as many tiny dots of ink forming a long row or line, and then another line next to it, and so on.

Eureka!

Computer printers for home use were developed in the 1960s. The print head had a grid-like set or matrix of tiny pins that pressed an inked ribbon onto paper, similar to old typewriter technology. This was called the dot-matrix printer. It could only produce marks the colour of the ribbon.

Whatever next?

Skin printers are small rollers that squirt out ink as they pass over the skin. They make images of any kind, usually from washable inks – like having an almost instant temporary tattoo.

There are two main types of design for inkjet print heads. In the fixed-head version the nozzles are permanent and need cleaning occasionally. In the disposable head type a new set of nozzles comes with each cartridge of ink or toner.

Rollers Driven by an electric motor, the roller system moves the paper past the print head a strip at a time and the print head produced each strip of the image.

Cover

Output

✳ 3D magic

Instead of the usual two-dimensional or 2D printing on a flat surface, 3D printing builds up solid objects layer by layer, with depth or height as the third dimension. A powder spreads out in the printer chamber, then a laser warms it only in the area of the print, so its particles stick together. The next layer is added on top, and as the same happens, this layer also fuses to the one below. When the layering is complete, the loose powder is removed. This method is used for 'fabbing' or prefabricating – making models and prototypes of complex shapes.

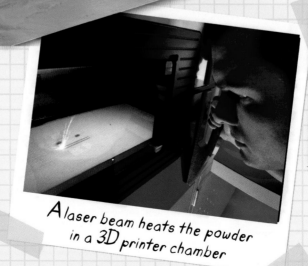

A laser beam heats the powder in a 3D printer chamber

Output tray Printed sheets pile up here. It is wise to let them dry separately, uncovered, where air can get to the ink. Otherwise they may smudge as they slide and press together.

Read more information on how printers work by visiting
www.factsforprojects.com and clicking on the web link.

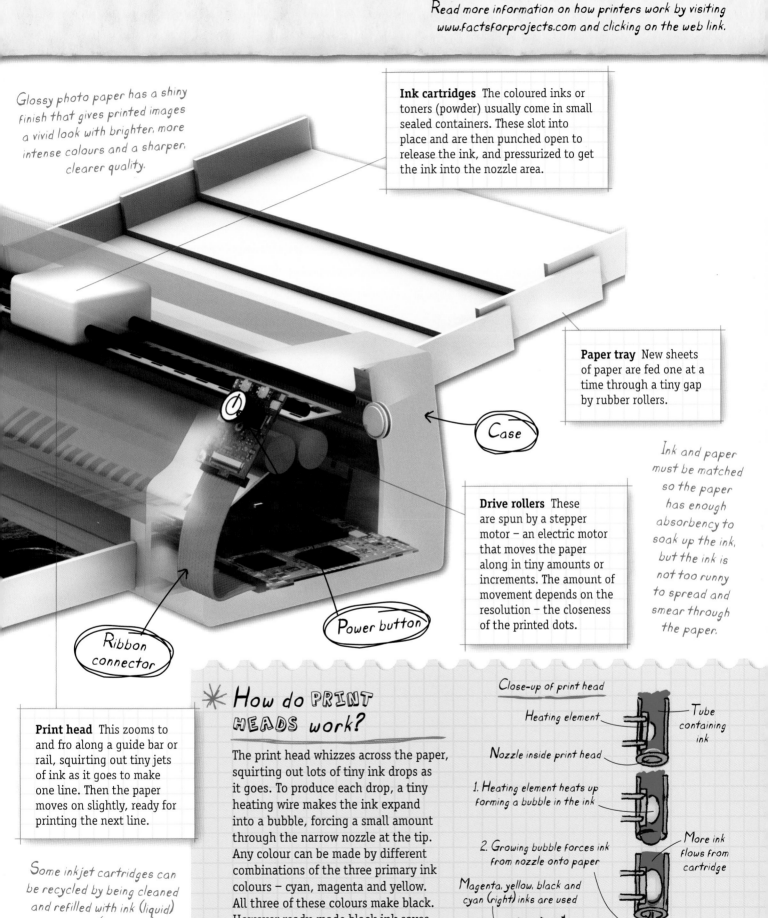

Glossy photo paper has a shiny finish that gives printed images a vivid look with brighter, more intense colours and a sharper, clearer quality.

Ink cartridges The coloured inks or toners (powder) usually come in small sealed containers. These slot into place and are then punched open to release the ink, and pressurized to get the ink into the nozzle area.

Paper tray New sheets of paper are fed one at a time through a tiny gap by rubber rollers.

Case

Ink and paper must be matched so the paper has enough absorbency to soak up the ink, but the ink is not too runny to spread and smear through the paper.

Drive rollers These are spun by a stepper motor – an electric motor that moves the paper along in tiny amounts or increments. The amount of movement depends on the resolution – the closeness of the printed dots.

Power button

Ribbon connector

Print head This zooms to and fro along a guide bar or rail, squirting out tiny jets of ink as it goes to make one line. Then the paper moves on slightly, ready for printing the next line.

Some inkjet cartridges can be recycled by being cleaned and refilled with ink (liquid) or toner (particles).

✳ How do PRINT HEADS work?

The print head whizzes across the paper, squirting out lots of tiny ink drops as it goes. To produce each drop, a tiny heating wire makes the ink expand into a bubble, forcing a small amount through the narrow nozzle at the tip. Any colour can be made by different combinations of the three primary ink colours – cyan, magenta and yellow. All three of these colours make black. However ready-made black ink saves using up the coloured inks.

Close-up of print head

Heating element

Tube containing ink

Nozzle inside print head

1. Heating element heats up forming a bubble in the ink

More ink flows from cartridge

2. Growing bubble forces ink from nozzle onto paper

Magenta, yellow, black and cyan (right) inks are used

RADIO MICROPHONE

A microphone changes patterns of sound waves into similar patterns of tiny electrical signals, which are fed into an amplifier to make them stronger. The long wire trailing from an ordinary microphone to the amplifier means that performers cannot move about with freedom – and they might even trip over it. The radio microphone sends its signals to the amplifier by radio waves.

Eureka!

The first microphones were in the first telephones, made by Alexander Graham Bell and his co-workers in the 1870s. By the 1920s bigger, better microphones were in regular use for radio broadcasts.

Whatever next?

A small pellet-like microphone can be placed in a false tooth to transmit what you say by radio – but you have to turn it down when you eat!

Performers often check a microphone by saying 'testing, one, two'. These words contain common voice sounds, such as 'sss' and a hard 't'.

Body or barrel

Batteries The barrel or main body of the microphone is shaped for grip in the hand and so is ideal for housing the batteries. A warning light shines when battery power begins to fade. To save the batteries the mike can be switched to 'mute', which means it goes silent but is ready for use again in an instant.

Transmitter and antenna The radio transmitter sends out coded radio waves from its antenna (aerial), carrying the sound information to a receiver that is usually less than 100 metres away.

Hand grip

In a hospital, a Bluetooth microphone links by radio to its base next door

✳ What is BLUETOOTH?

To avoid too many tangled and trailing wires, electrical devices can send information between themselves using radio waves, known as 'wireless'. Bluetooth is not the name of a particular make or type of device. It is the 'label' for the way the information is coded into radio signals, and a standard for the speed, quality, strength and reliability of the short-range wireless system. All Bluetooth devices can communicate or 'talk' to each other in the standard way, rather than different manufacturers using their own systems that did not communicate.

'Bugs' are small listening devices made up of a tiny microphone and radio transmitter. They are often used for spying and secret investigations.

Find out more information about different types of microphone by visiting www.factsforprojects.com and clicking on the web link.

As well as moving-coil microphones there are many other kinds including condenser, laser, electrostatic, carbon-granule and piezoelectric mikes. Each has its own benefits, such as light weight, durability or high quality sound reproduction.

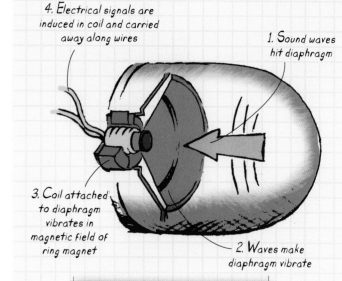

4. Electrical signals are induced in coil and carried away along wires

1. Sound waves hit diaphragm

3. Coil attached to diaphragm vibrates in magnetic field of ring magnet

2. Waves make diaphragm vibrate

How do MICROPHONES work?

There are many kinds of microphones. Many in regular stage use are called dynamic or moving-coil mikes and work by the process of electromagnetic induction. Sound waves make a wire coil vibrate within a magnetic field. This movement of a wire near a magnet causes, or induces, electrical currents to flow in the wire. The pattern of the current is the same as the pattern of sound waves. The opposite process, known as the electromagnetic effect, is used in a loudspeaker (see page 24).

Permanent magnet

Magnetic coil The coil attached to the diaphragm is wound from many turns of ultra-thin wire. The more turns it has, the stronger the electrical signals it generates, and so the clearer the sounds are.

A unidirectional microphone picks up sounds from only one direction.

Muffler or guard A foam cover over the diaphragm prevents the wind and air currents from rattling the diaphragm. But at the same it is acoustically transparent, allowing through sound waves from the air around.

PCBs Printed circuit boards filter, convert and clean up the electrical signals from the wire coil, ready to feed to the transmitter.

Head

Diaphragm The thin, flexible diaphragm shakes very fast, or vibrates, when sound waves bounce off it. This makes the wire coil attached to it vibrate with a similar pattern of movements.

An omnidirectional mike detects sounds from all directions.

LOUDSPEAKERS

A loudspeaker or 'speaker' turns electrical signals into corresponding patterns of sound waves – the opposite of a microphone (see page 22). To make the electrical signals strong enough to power a loudspeaker, they usually have to be boosted or increased by an amplifier or 'amp'.

Eureka!

Like early microphones, the first loudspeakers were developed by Alexander Graham Bell and his colleagues for the first telephones, during the 1870s.

Whatever next?

Tiny Bluetooth-type radio earphones could be implanted into the human ear and activated by brainwaves. It may then be possible to switch on a radio link and listen just by thinking.

The massive speakers at big events need thousands of watts of power, while the tiny ones in earphones need just a few thousandths of a watt.

Unlike many modern electronic devices, loudspeakers are analogue. They use electrical signals of varying strength rather than on–off digital signals.

Coil The wire coil inside the magnet, also known as the voice coil, has many turns of very thin wire. This makes it move as much as possible even with very weak electrical signals

Ring magnet

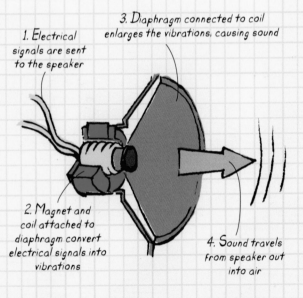

1. Electrical signals are sent to the speaker

3. Diaphragm connected to coil enlarges the vibrations, causing sound

2. Magnet and coil attached to diaphragm convert electrical signals into vibrations

4. Sound travels from speaker out into air

✳ How do MOVING-COIL LOUDSPEAKERS work?

A loudspeaker uses the opposite principle to electromagnetic induction, which is known as the electromagnetic effect. When an electric current passes through a wire coil, this becomes an electromagnet with its own magnetic field. In a speaker the field interacts with the constant field of a ring-shaped permanent magnet around it, alternately pulling (attraction) and pushing (repulsion). This makes the coil vibrate, which it passes its vibrations to the diaphragm, which then produces the sound waves.

Stand

Diaphragm Also called the cone, this is usually made of stiff plastic or specially treated card. It has a flexible outer rim so it can vibrate freely within its frame.

Carry out a simple activity and learn more about making and hearing sounds by visiting www.factsforprojects.com and clicking on the web link.

The name 'loudspeaker' can be used for the box, cabinet or container housing one or more actual speaker units, which are then known as 'drivers'.

✳ Tiny SPEAKERS

Earphones are tiny loudspeakers, small enough to fit in the ear. The magnets in earphones are made of special alloys, or combinations of metals that have a very strong magnetic field but are also light and not damaged by knocks and vibrations. These alloys include the rare metals samarium and cobalt, which make earphones with powerful low frequencies for a deep bass sound. Headphones have slightly larger speakers and padded cups that fit over the ears to keep out unwanted sounds.

Earphones let us listen without disturbing others too much

Tweeter This smaller loudspeaker produces shrill notes or high frequencies such as cymbals and the 'sss' sounds of the voice.

Subwoofer loudspeakers or subs produce some sound waves that are too deep or low for the human ear to detect. However we can 'feel' them in our bodies as a deep thud or thump.

Grill A protective covering stops damage to the loudspeaker or driver unit but lets sound waves pass through unaffected.

iPod

Dock

Woofer The larger loudspeaker produces deep notes or low frequencies such as drums and bass guitars.

Apart from moving-coil or dynamic loudspeakers there are also electrostatic, ribbon and piezoelectric (crystal-based) types for special applications.

Some very high-quality loudspeaker systems have five driver units for different frequencies or pitches of sound: subwoofer, woofer, midrange, tweeter and ultratweeter.

Now Playing

1 of 14

Dani California
Red Hot Chili Peppers
Stadium Arcadium

3:27 -1:15

MENU

PERSONAL MUSIC PLAYER

Various manufacturers make portable personal music players, also called digital audio players. Those produced by Apple are called iPods, while many others are known by the general name of MP3 players. The term 'MP3' refers to the way the sounds are changed into digital code and 'compressed' to take up less memory space without loss of quality.

Eureka!

The iPod took little more than one year to develop, under the close eye of Apple chief Steve Jobs. It was launched in 2001 with the catchphrase '1000 songs in your pocket' and has been a best seller ever since.

Whatever next?

MP4 is faster to transfer than MP3, works with audio and video, takes up even less memory and is more suitable for streaming (transferring 'live' in real time) over the Internet.

MP3 stands for mpeg audio layer 3. The 'mpeg' part is Moving Pictures Expert Group. It refers to a team of electronics experts who worked out how images and sounds could be changed into digital electronic form using a series of mathematical sums and formulas known as algorithms.

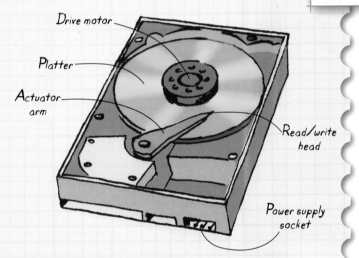

Drive motor
Platter
Actuator arm
Read/write head
Power supply socket

Battery pack

Display The LCD screen shows menus of choices, which song is playing, earphone volume and many other features.

Slim case

iPod
Music
Videos
Photos
Podcasts
Extras
Settings
Shuffle S
Now Pla

TOSHIBA
DISK DRIVE
HDD1422
S/N74U4782

Hard drive This mini-version of a computer hard disc stores all the audio information, usually measured in gigabytes or GB of memory space.

How does a HARD DRIVE work?

A hard drive (hard disc) is one or a stack of spinning discs or platters, each coated with a very thin layer of magnetic substance. Read-write heads on arms swivel over the disc surface, hardly touching. They write information in specific places by creating patterns of magnetic spots, or read information by detecting these spots.

Shockproofing The hard drive in a digital player is tough. But it is also covered by rubber strips or similar packing to cushion it from knocks and jolts.

Discover everything you need to know about MP3 players by visiting www.factsforprojects.com and clicking on the web link.

EXPLODED VIEW OF APPLE iPOD

Some digital music players with display screens have video games such as Brick, Solitaire and Music Quiz.

Flash memory is non-volatile, which means it doesn't need an electricity supply to 'refresh' or maintain it. It should stay in a microchip for years with no electrical power.

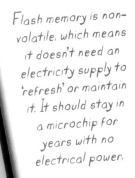

Album artwork

MENU

Motherboard

✳ FLASHY MEMORY

Some MP3 players use flash memory, which is a microchip that holds information that can be deleted and reprogrammed. Flash memory chips or 'sticks' are smaller and cheaper than a tiny hard drive or microdrive, but hold less information. However they also use less electricity and so allow batteries to last longer than with a microdrive. Most flash chips are protected in plastic cases and plug into the USB (universal serial bus) socket of a player, computer or network.

The USB memory stick plugs into many electronic devices

Click wheel Play and pause, skip forwards or back, volume, choose a menu item, and return to the previous menu are carried out by pressing or stroking parts of this wheel, rather than by pressing a row of buttons.

The forerunner of the iPod/MP3 player was the portable laser-based CD player. It was more than ten times bigger and heavier than an MP3 player. Moving it often made the compact disc skip.

Touch-sensors A series of flat components called capacitors detects when an object, such as a finger, is near and which way it moves. The presence of the object alters the amount of electricity that the capacitor can hold.

VIDEO GAMES CONSOLE

Computer games consoles and video games machines have been around since the 1960s. Early versions had just a few games, like 'tennis' with two bats and a ball – in black and white! The latest consoles have hundreds of games in stunning fast-action 3D colour. You can play yourself, or against friends, or online with someone on the other side of the world.

Eureka!

The first computer game using graphics – pictures and symbols rather than words – was noughts-and-crosses in 1952. 'Tennis' followed in 1958, and the first true computer game SpaceWar! arrived in 1962.

Whatever next?

Some people say video games should have built-in 'rest periods' where the game stops for ten minutes every hour, for health reasons and to prevent people getting obsessed.

SONY PLAYSTATION

One of the most popular games ever was Space Invaders. It was launched in 1978 in video gaming arcades and then for home machines. No other arcade game has been played so much.

Main board

✳ Virtual WORLDS

Video 'games' on the Internet have become so detailed and complex that they are almost like leading an alternative existence in the virtual world of computing. Avatars (a name derived from the Hindu religion) are characters or representations that gamers use for themselves, varying from human-like forms to animals, monsters, robots, machines or simple symbols or icons.

Chips The many microchips include a clock chip that ensures all the circuits work together properly and signals are sent between them on time.

Video games consoles are now in the seventh generation with models such as the Sony PlayStation 3, Microsoft Xbox 360 and Nintendo Wii.

Gamers gather at big meetings to play the latest releases

Optical disc drive Advanced games machines can play DVDs and Blu-ray discs, and so be used as a disc player to watch movies on a high-definition (HD) television or computer display.

PLAYSTATION

Find out everything you need to know about video games and consoles by visiting www.factsforprojects.com and clicking on the web link.

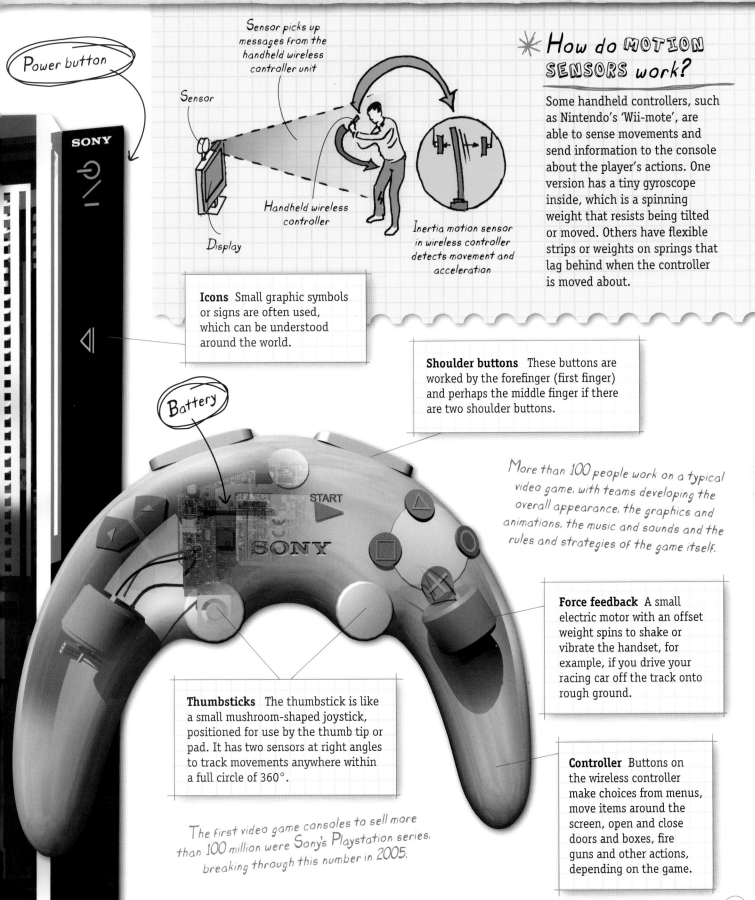

Power button

SONY

Sensor picks up messages from the handheld wireless controller unit

Sensor

Handheld wireless controller

Display

Inertia motion sensor in wireless controller detects movement and acceleration

✳ **How do MOTION SENSORS work?**

Some handheld controllers, such as Nintendo's 'Wii-mote', are able to sense movements and send information to the console about the player's actions. One version has a tiny gyroscope inside, which is a spinning weight that resists being tilted or moved. Others have flexible strips or weights on springs that lag behind when the controller is moved about.

Icons Small graphic symbols or signs are often used, which can be understood around the world.

Battery

Shoulder buttons These buttons are worked by the forefinger (first finger) and perhaps the middle finger if there are two shoulder buttons.

SELECT   START

SONY

More than 100 people work on a typical video game, with teams developing the overall appearance, the graphics and animations, the music and sounds and the rules and strategies of the game itself.

Force feedback A small electric motor with an offset weight spins to shake or vibrate the handset, for example, if you drive your racing car off the track onto rough ground.

Thumbsticks The thumbstick is like a small mushroom-shaped joystick, positioned for use by the thumb tip or pad. It has two sensors at right angles to track movements anywhere within a full circle of 360°.

Controller Buttons on the wireless controller make choices from menus, move items around the screen, open and close doors and boxes, fire guns and other actions, depending on the game.

The first video game consoles to sell more than 100 million were Sony's Playstation series, breaking through this number in 2005.

HOME CINEMA

A trip to the real cinema is an exciting event, to watch the new blockbuster movie on the big screen with loud sound all around. But in the past 20 years home cinemas have become bigger and better. The key parts are a widescreen display or television, a sound system with several loudspeakers, and the movie itself, usually on a DVD player.

Eureka!

The first CDs were sold in the early 1980s. They were used for audio (sound), usually recorded music. Computer engineers then used them to store words, pictures and software, applications or programs, and data files. In recent years they have been partly replaced for data storage by devices such as mini hard drives, microdrives and memory cards, chips or sticks.

Whatever next?

Scientists are in the process of developing holographic displays where the scenes and objects are projected as coloured lights in three dimensions, including true depth rather than the illusion of depth on a flat screen.

Blu-ray discs look like bluish versions of a CD or DVD. They use blue laser light, which can read tinier spots than the usual red DVD laser. This enables the Blu-ray disc to hold more information – 25 or even 50 GB, for movies in HD (high-definition).

Speakers In a standard 5:1 loudspeaker set-up there is one subwoofer for very deep sounds that can be positioned almost anywhere, left and right front speakers for stereo effect, a central front speaker to 'fill the gap' for sounds coming from the middle, and left and right rear speakers for 'surround sound'.

Many modern smash-hit movies such as WALL-E use CGI

✳ SUPER-REAL

Many spectacular films use CGI, computer generated images, either for special effects amid real-life action or for an entire animated movie. Characters and scenes are built up as three-dimensional net-like 'meshes' in computer memory, showing their basic shapes. The meshes can be manipulated and changed according to mathematical rules, such as when a character walks along.

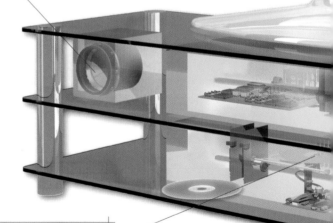

DVD player A standard DVD holds about 4.7 GB (gigabytes), which is up to six times more information than a CD. That's enough for colour pictures and sound for more than two hours of movie.

The first cinema screening was in Paris, France, in 1895. Brothers August and Louis Lumière showed ten 50-second films they had made, including one of workers leaving their factory.

For a complete guide to home cinema systems visit www.factsforprojects.com and click on the web link.

Wide screen The wide screen format of 16:9 (see page 10) has the correct proportions of width to height to fit neatly in our field of vision – the complete area we can see with both eyes.

Component shelving

Connecting cables There are several types of connecting cables including elongated 21-pin SCART plugs, component video leads with red, green and blue plugs, small round S-video plugs, DVI (Digital Visual Interface) plugs as used for computer monitors, and the latest 19-pin HDMI (High-Definition Multimedia Interface) design.

✳ How do CDs and DVDs work?

Compact discs and digital versatile (or video) discs are optical – they use light. Each disc has a spiral track of tiny hollows or pits with flat areas, called lands, between. The sequence of pits and lands contains the digitally coded information. As the disc spins, a laser beam reflects off the pits but not the lands. The flashes of reflection are picked up by a detector.

3. Laser light is reflected back by pits on disc but not by lands

Disc

Lenses

2. Beam splitter allows light from the laser to pass through to the disc but bounces the reflected light from the disc through the lens to the detector

Multibeam detector

Lens

Laser

1. As disc spins, whole laser reader moves from centre of disc outwards to follow the spiral track

Sound system Audio information from the DVD is fed into the sound system, which has controls such as volume (loudness), bass (deep notes), treble (high notes), balance (left or right speakers) and fade (front to rear speakers).

VIRTUAL REALITY

Reality is real. Virtuality is not – but it seems real to our senses such as vision, hearing and touch. The best virtual reality or VR systems feed information such as sights, sounds and movements to the human brain and trick it into believing that things are real and actually exist, rather than being artificial or 'pretend'. VR can be used for fun and entertainment, and for serious purposes such as training pilots to fly and surgeons to carry out medical operations.

Eureka!

Some of the first VR machines were flight simulators for pilots and air crew. In World War II (1939–1945) the Celestial Navigation Trainer, a massive machine at 13.7 metres high, could hold an entire bomber aircraft crew training for night-time missions.

Whatever next?

As VR equipment becomes faster and more complicated, more body senses can be stimulated. Tiny pellets of different odours can be released from the headset, for example, the smell of smoke when training firefighters to tackle a virtual inferno.

Screens Two screens give slightly different views of the scene, just like human eyes. The brain merges these into one three-dimensional view.

The Virtual Cocoon Room stimulates all the senses to take the person on a tour of anywhere in the world, from the African grasslands to a deep cave.

Earphones Stereo sound is played through the earphones or headphones. Action that looks as if it is happening to the left of the wearer is accompanied by sounds that are louder in the left earpiece.

✳ VIRTUALLY FLYING

Full motion flight simulators not only show a widescreen view of what is outside, which changes according to which way the pilot guides the 'aircraft'. The simulator or 'sim' also leans, tilts and shakes using powerful, fast-acting hydraulic pistons underneath, to recreate the movements of the aircraft. It can make a beginner feel very airsick!

Pilots train in a Boeing flight simulator

Virtual surgery can be extended into tele-surgery or remote surgery, where a surgeon in one place works a console that controls robot equipment operating on the patient in another place.

Play an on-line flight simulation game by visiting www.factsforprojects.com and clicking on the web link.

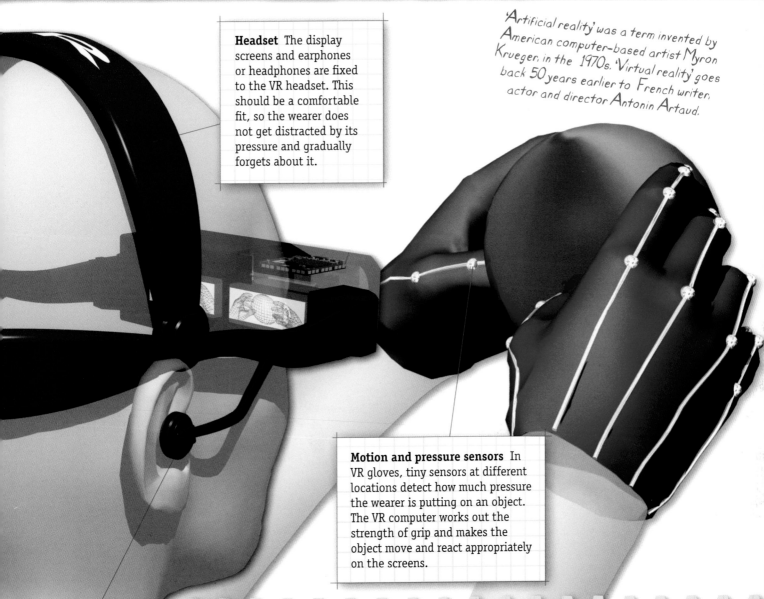

Headset The display screens and earphones or headphones are fixed to the VR headset. This should be a comfortable fit, so the wearer does not get distracted by its pressure and gradually forgets about it.

'Artificial reality' was a term invented by American computer-based artist Myron Krueger, in the 1970s. 'Virtual reality' goes back 50 years earlier to French writer, actor and director Antonin Artaud.

Motion and pressure sensors In VR gloves, tiny sensors at different locations detect how much pressure the wearer is putting on an object. The VR computer works out the strength of grip and makes the object move and react appropriately on the screens.

Wireless link The VR headset, gloves and perhaps even a whole body suit are linked by radio to the main console, so that the wearer can move and react freely.

The first VR headsets were built in the late 1960s. They were so heavy that they had to be hung from a frame above to avoid crushing the wearer!

✳ How does STEREO VISION work?

Human eyes each see a slightly different view of the world, known as stereoscopic vision. The closer an object, the more different these views. By comparing them, the brain works out the distance of the object. A VR headset's screens show two different views, one for each eye, with no area of overlap as when looking at a normal TV screen. The brain combines the separate views so that objects look and 'feel' as if they are near or far.

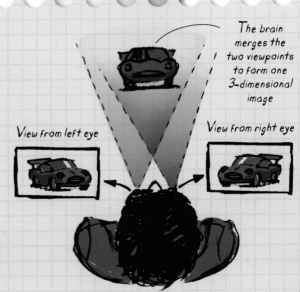

The brain merges the two viewpoints to form one 3-dimensional image

View from left eye

View from right eye

MOBILE PHONE

It's hard to imagine life without the 'mobile' or cellphone. Yet just 20 years ago these handy gadgets were three times bigger and cost five times more – and text messaging was almost unknown. Today's models do not so much shrink in size, as they did in the past. Rather they pack in more and more functions, such as games, camera, video and sound recording, satnav, Bluetooth short-range wireless link, Internet access, music player, radio and television.

Eureka!

In the 1980s, early 'mobile' phones were the size of house bricks and just as heavy. Apart from progress in microchips and radio circuits, one of the main advances has been batteries that are smaller and lighter but last many times longer.

Whatever next?

Technically it is possible to make a mobile phone smaller than your little finger. However the screen, icons and buttons would be too small to see or manipulate. Advances in voice control may overcome this problem.

In 2008 about two mobile phones in every five sold were made by Nokia.

EXPLODED VIEW OF APPLE iPHONE

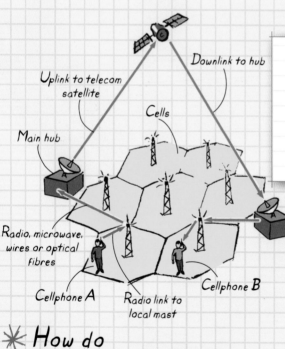

Uplink to telecom satellite

Downlink to hub

Cells

Main hub

Radio, microwave, wires or optical fibres

Cellphone A

Radio link to local mast

Cellphone B

Icons An icon is a small picture, image or symbol representing information or a particular function such as 'Send text message'.

✳ How do CELLPHONES work?

Each area or cell has a radio transmitter-receiver mast that regularly sends out its identification code. A cellphone detects the strongest code and sends outgoing talk or text messages to it. The mast links by radio, microwaves or wires to a main hub, which communicates with the whole telecom network including satellites. The network finds the receiver cellphone and sends the message to the nearest mast – which could be in the next cell!

In clear, flat, open areas, a typical mobile phone has a range of about 40 km to the nearest transmitter-receiver mast.

NiMH cell The nickel-metal hydride cell is a small but powerful and long-lasting rechargeable battery. Larger versions power electric cars and trucks.

Discover how mobile phones send and receive calls by visiting
www.factsforprojects.com and clicking on the web link.

In areas of great natural beauty, cellphone transmitter-receiver masts may be disguised as trees, so as not to ruin the view.

Texting is convenient and cheaper than making calls

✳ WHY TEXT?

SMS, Short Message Service, carries information of up to 160 characters – numbers, letters and symbols such as & and @. A text takes only a split second to send and is cheaper than talking. Also you do not hold the phone to your ear, where some people worry that the radio waves it transmits could damage the ear or even the brain. Medical tests so far show that there is no evidence of harm from using a mobile phone.

Protective screen

Touch screen The touch screen does away with physical buttons on the phone interface by showing button icons to press. This is more adaptable, being able to change the button icons according to the phone's mode, such as address book, gaming or texting.

On/off/sleep The main power button puts the phone into energy-saving 'sleep' mode when pressed, and turns the phone on or off when held down for a longer time.

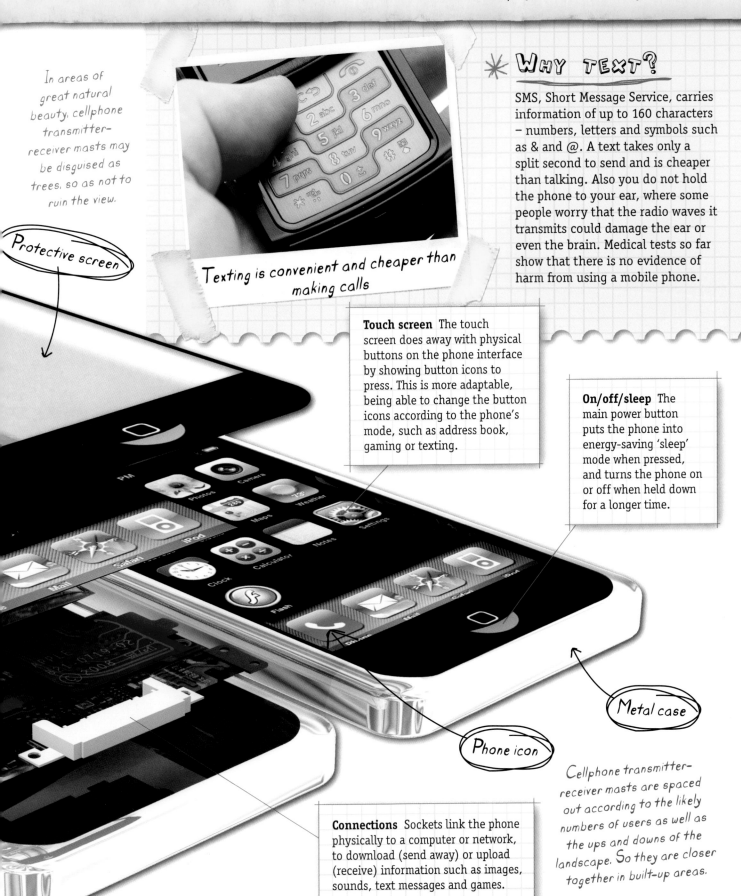

Metal case

Phone icon

Connections Sockets link the phone physically to a computer or network, to download (send away) or upload (receive) information such as images, sounds, text messages and games.

Cellphone transmitter-receiver masts are spaced out according to the likely numbers of users as well as the ups and downs of the landscape. So they are closer together in built-up areas.

SATELLITE NAVIGATION SYSTEM

Satellite navigation describes the use of a GPS receiver to pinpoint or 'fix' your location, and navigate your way from place to place. GPS is the Global Positioning System – a network of about 30 satellites 22,200 kilometres high in space, orbiting the Earth twice daily – plus the radio links, computers and other equipment that control and co-ordinate them. A GPS receiver detects signals from the satellites and displays its own position or location on a screen.

Eureka!

The first global navigation system was Transit in the 1960s. It had five satellites, took two minutes to make a 'fix' and had a best accuracy of about 100 metres.

Whatever next?

The USA developed the main GPS we use today, but other nations and groups are building their own systems. These include China's Compass, Russia's Glosnass and India's IRNSS. The European Union, in partnership with several other countries, is developing the Galileo GPS.

In some cars with tinted windows and heated windscreens, the metal in the tints and heating elements can prevent satellite radio signals from reaching the GPS unit inside.

Changes high in the Earth's atmosphere, especially in the layer called the ionosphere (from 50 to 1000 km) can bend or weaken GPS satellite signals. Making corrections for this problem is a big challenge for GPS designers.

Batteries

Receiver The receiver unit compares the available satellite signals and 'locks on' to the three strongest or most suitable ones.

Components Among the many chips inside, SIDRAM (synchronous dynamic random access memory) holds temporary information that can be changed fast. It is linked or 'synched' to the other components so that it supplies its information almost instantly on demand. In a GPS receiver, fractions of thousandths of a second are very important.

✳ How does GPS work?

At any place on Earth's surface, a GPS receiver can 'see' in a clear line three or more of the system's satellites, high above in space, and so receive signals from them. Each satellite continuously transmits its own identity and also the exact time. Radio waves go fast, but there is a slight time difference between them reaching the receiver, because they are different distances from it. The receiver works out the delay in time from each satellite and compares them, to know its distance from them and so work out its own position on Earth's surface.

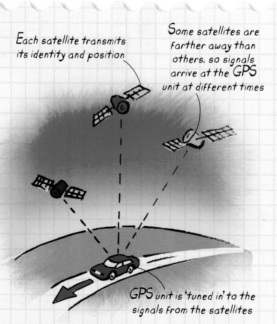

Each satellite transmits its identity and position

Some satellites are farther away than others, so signals arrive at the GPS unit at different times

GPS unit is 'tuned in' to the signals from the satellites

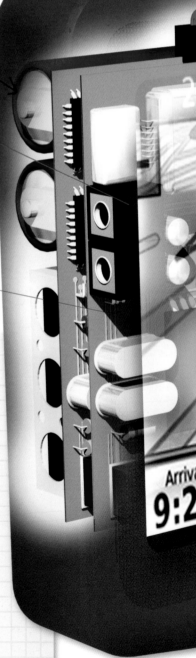

Arrival
9:2

Read extra information and watch an animation about GPS by visiting www.factsforprojects.com and clicking on the web links.

Antenna (aerial) As well as an in-built antenna, the wires that connect the unit to an electricity supply may also be used to receive radio signals. The circuits are designed to detect radio signals from all available GPS satellites, and to minimize the signals from other sources such as television, radio and mobile phone networks.

DGPS is used to map a glacier and follow global warming

✳ NEVER LOST AGAIN

As the name 'global' suggests, GPS works anywhere in the world – even in frozen polar wastes or on remote mountaintops, where there is no mobile phone network. Its accuracy depends partly on the cost of the receiver, with its complex circuits to compare satellite signals, but is usually to within a few metres. Even better accuracy is obtained from a receiver that can also detect radio signals from one or more transmitters on land, known as DGPS, differential GPS.

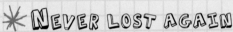

Anti-glare touch screen

Speaker Most GPS units can 'talk' using pre-recorded words to give instructions such as 'At the next road junction, turn left'. On many receivers there is a choice of voices and accents.

The main GPS was developed by the USA for military use, with secretly coded satellite signals. It was made available to anyone by altering the codes following a terrible aircraft disaster in 1983 when 269 people died.

Case

Screen The LCD colour display can show various images, often a road map of the area showing direction of travel with the receiver at the lower centre.

GLOSSARY

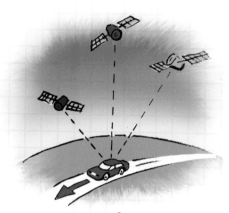

Satellite navigation system

Alloy

A combination of metals, or metals and other substances, for special purposes such as great strength, extreme lightness, resistance to high temperatures, or all of these.

Analogue

Signals that carry information or data by varying in strength or size, such as by the varying strength (voltage) of an electric current.

Antenna

Part of a communications system that sends out and/or receives radio signals, microwaves or similar waves. Most antenna, also called aerials, are either long and thin like wires, bar-shaped, or dish-shaped like a bowl.

Atmosphere

The layer of gases – air – around a very large space object such as planet Earth.

Bluetooth

A wireless system for using radio waves to communicate and send information over relatively short distances, usually tens of metres.

Blu-ray

A type of optical (light-based) disc, similar to a DVD, which uses blue laser light. This has shorter waves compared to the usual red DVD laser and so it can read smaller pits on the disc. This enables a Blu-ray disc to hold more information than a standard DVD – up to 50 GB (gigabytes).

CCD

Charge-coupled device, a microchip that turns patterns of light rays into patterns of electronic signals.

CD

Compact disc, a plastic-based disc usually 12 centimetres across, with a very thin metal layer. This layer stores information or data in the form of microscopic pits, which are detected or 'read' by a laser beam. Most CDs have a memory capacity of 650–750 MB (megabytes).

Digital

Carrying information or data in the form of coded on-off signals, usually millions every second.

DVD

Digital versatile disc (sometimes digital 'video' disc), a plastic-based disc usually 12 centimetres across, with a very thin metal layer. This stores information or data in the form of microscopic pits, which are detected or 'read' by a laser beam. Most DVDs have a memory capacity of 4.7 GB or 4700 MB. Double-sided dual-layer versions can hold more than 17 GB.

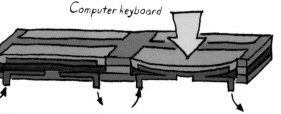

Computer keyboard

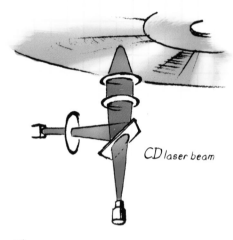

CD laser beam

Electrode

An electrical contact, or part of an electrical pathway or circuit, that is either positive (+) or negative (−).

Electron

Tiny particles inside atoms with a negative electrical charge or force, which move around the central area (nucleus) of the atom. Lots of electrons moving along between atoms make an electric current.

Frequency

How often something happens over a certain unit of time, usually one second. For example, low-frequency sound waves vibrate about 50–100 times each second.

Gears

Toothed wheels or sprockets that fit or mesh together so that one turns the other. If they are connected by a chain or belt with holes where the teeth fit, they are generally called sprockets. Gears are used to change turning speed and force and to alter turning direction.

Giga-

One thousand million, as in 1 GB (gigabyte), which is 1,000,000,000 bytes of information or data. For a typical MP3 digital music player, 1 GB is about 16 hours of sound.

Gyroscope

A device that maintains its position and resists being moved or tilted because of its movement energy. It can be used to measure speed and direction of movement. It usually consists of a very fast-spinning ball or wheel in a frame.

HD

High definition, in screen technology, where the tiny coloured spots or pixels are smaller and closer than on a normal screen, to show more fine detail.

Infrared

A form of energy, as rays or waves, which is similar to light but with longer waves that have a heating effect.

Kilo-

One thousand, as in 1 KB (kilobyte), which is 1000 bytes of information or data. For a typical MP3 digital music player, 1 KB is about one-sixteenth of one second of sound.

Laser

A special high-energy form of light that is only one pure colour. All of its waves are exactly the same length, and they are parallel to each other rather than spreading out as in normal light.

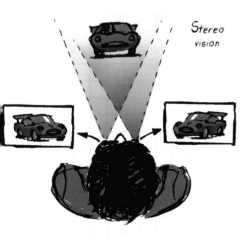

Stereo vision

Microphone

LCD

Liquid crystal display, a technology for showing images on screen using semi-liquid crystals that 'twist' or polarize light rays.

Lens

A shaped piece of clear glass, plastic or a similar transparent substance that bends or refracts light rays. It changes their direction so that they either come together or converge, or spread apart or diverge.

Mega-

One million, as in 1 MB (megabyte), which is 1,000,000 bytes of information or data. For a typical MP3 digital music player, 1 MB is about one minute of sound.

Microchip

A small sliver or 'chip' of a substance, usually silicon or germanium. It has many microscopic electronic components and devices, such as resistors and transistors, built into it.

Optical

Working with light rays, instead of other waves or rays (such as radio waves, microwaves or infrared 'heat' rays).

Orbit

A curved path around a larger object, such as a satellite going around Earth, or the Earth orbiting around the Sun.

Pixels

Picture elements, the tiny spots or areas of different colours and brightness that together make up a bigger picture or image.

Plasma

A substance similar to a gas, but where its tiniest particles (atoms) get extremely hot and have an electric charge and lots of energy.

Radio waves

Invisible waves of combined electricity and magnetism where each wave is quite long, from a few millimetres to many kilometres. (Light waves are similar but much shorter in length.)

Satellite

Any object that goes around or orbits another. For example, the Moon is a natural satellite of the Earth. The term is used especially for artificial or man-made orbiting objects, particularly those going around the Earth.

Satnav

Satellite navigation, finding your way and location using radio signals from the GPS (Global Positioning System) satellites in space.

Solar

To do with the Sun.

Solar panel

A device that turns sunlight directly into electricity, as used in many small gadgets and also on satellites.

Wireless

When electronic devices can communicate or transfer information without wires, usually by waves such as radio, microwaves or infrared rays.

INDEX